Thank you for selecting this book. We are a
company — a consortium of educators, boc
parents, and kid-teste

MW01493036

PreK Lab

Leave us a quick review on our website and receive free assessment test!

The PreK Lab Team
www.preklab.com

PreKLab.com. All rights reserved. No part of this book may be reproduced or distributed by any means or in any form. It may not be stored in any retrieval system or database without obtaining the prior written approval of **PreKLab.com**.

PreKLab.com is not liable for the accuracy of this content nor is it liable for errors or for omissions of any form. **PreKLab.com** publishes all material without any kind of warranty, implied or express. **PreKLab.com** is not responsible for any damage or loss that may be caused by a reader/customer retying on the information in **PreKLab.com** published material. All information is subject to change without notice.

INTRODUCTION

Help toddlers get ready for reading, writing, and numbers! This book introduces reasoning exercises, problem-solving tasks, and cognitive skill-building activities to young children through kid-friendly subjects. This activity book is a collection of learning activities that have been carefully selected to appeal to kids aged 1 to 3. Age-appropriateness is an important factor in choosing learning tools.

This toddler workbook for 1 year and up is an engaging mix of mazes, matching games, picture puzzles and more-keep kids thoroughly entertained while they learn important, age-appropriate skills from focus and fine motor coordination to problem solving and social skills.
- This workbook offers fun, kid-friendly themes to engage children.
- The exercises are meant to be done together with no time limit.

Find the products from the list

Which is the smallest?

Draw a line to match each object to its shadow

Find the differences

Help policeman
to catch the thief

Can you find the matching shoes?

Help children to find their table. The shape in the child's hands matches the shape under the table.

Match a car with a driver

Sample

Cut and glue the flower

Can you find these hidden objects?

Circle the things that belongs to doctor

How many kittens do you see?

Enter the code
to lock the cell

425

Enter the code
to lock the cell

Find the differences

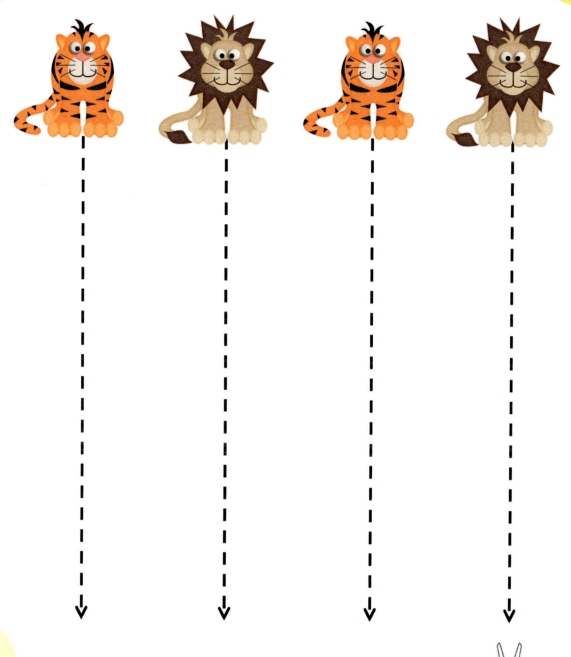

Cut along the dotted line

Match
and name shapes

Match
and name shapes

Which is the biggest?

Show the picture with 1 hedgehog

Find the differences

Trace the lines

Draw a line to match each object to its shadow

Can you find the matching mittens?

Help the children to find their homes. The homes' color matches to the color of children' cloth.

Match shapes

Match tails
to the animal

 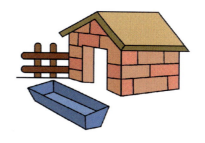

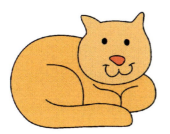 

 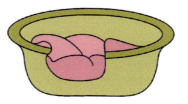

Match the animals to their homes

Help the bear to find his home.

Made in the USA
Monee, IL
29 January 2025

11246109R00031